House of Thanksgiving

a collection of poems by

Stuart Kestenbaum

PUBLISHED BY
Deerbrook Editions
P.O. Box 542
Cumberland, Maine 04021-0542

FIRST EDITION

ISBN number: 0-9712488-1-8

Manufactured by Sheridan Books, Inc.

Book Design by Jeffrey Haste
The typefaces used in this book are Spectrum, Goudy Sans, and Goudy Handtooled.
Spectrum was designed by Jan Van Krimpen.

for my brother Howard
1945-2001

Contents

III

IV

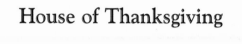
House of Thanksgiving

I

Cider

Lloyd knows all the trees on the island
the ones that were overgrown
but were once pruned and picked
for pies and cider, baking and eating.
The ones with the forgotten names—
Gravenstein, Northern Spy, Jonathan—
and the histories of the hardscrabble
homesteads they grew on.
Every year they were touched
by someone's hands in the fields and yards
where delicate blossoms come early
in the sudden New England spring.
He guides us to the cross road
near the cemetery back by the shed
once used for chickens
and now used for nothing.
Close by are the second growth spruce
where in early winter deer will
leap out to eat the fallen fruit.
But now we are the ones who crouch
in the tall grass of autumn's
fertility and decay and pick the drops,
the huge red Kings, an apple
almost gone from memory
nearly two bushels from one tree
that we add to our mix
of Macintosh and Golden Delicious.
In the colder afternoon air
Lloyd cranks the press down with an iron bar
turning pulp into cider
as yellow jackets swarm
and stumble around us, celebrating
the old sweetness as it goes by.

Post Office Box

The P.O. Box has seen so much of the world
without leaving 04627, its surface a patina of sorrow
left by starving children, the horrors of
the Klan and diseases that must be conquered.
Still there is always an opportunity to win millions
of dollars, in a letter that comes in your name
from your friend Ed McMahon. And look, there
are TVs to buy, chickens are on sale
and your septic system's life can be extended.
It has seen what is owed and what you owe.
It wants to tell you that Ed McMahon is not
really your friend, that he writes to everyone
that way, that you should be waiting for a
different kind of letter, something special
delivery saying "come home all is forgiven",
but to receive this you need to write letters
as if writing could save your life, letters
that say what you love, the envelopes with
the handwritten address, the first class postage.

Bangor Daily

E.B. White got it. Roger Angell gets it
in the summer and I believe that
Philip Booth reads it all year.
I join this brotherhood walking
to the green plastic tube
at the end of the driveway
the new snow and gray sky making
a blue light before sunrise.
I take heart reaching for
the frozen words, knowing
that I'm sharing the same paper
these great writers read.
I shake the newsprint free of snow
as the pick-ups drive by.
I am a simple man and take solace
in unscrambling the jumble, in
making words be what they need to be.
My angels of the advice column
give me comfort and Mark Trail moves
day by day in a forest without doubt.
What more could I need?
Nearly all the words are there
for the poems I need to write—
the verbs, the articles, the punctuation.
All those letters, all those pages,
all the way down the two-lane
road from Bangor it has traveled,
quietly slipped into homes in the dark.
The same dark before dawn I couldn't
sleep in last night and began to think
of others who join me in the space between
sleep and light, words and silence,
where our souls detach themselves from
our bodies and move inside us like
birds trapped inside a house,
the space we fill endlessly
with ourselves as if day would never break
bringing us the good news.

Birthday

I am not thinking of the grim reaper,
but I decide to cut the grass
on the first sunny day in a week
and the overgrown lawn, blown and creased
in furrows by the wind, is like
the rich grassland of a foreign place.
Where the leach field lies the grass is
a deep long green, thriving on
my waste, on the rich water of decay.
Above me barn swallows fight for
space on the wire. Are they getting
ready to nest, or have I released
their insect sustenance with my mowing?
Lupines are beginning to take over
at the edges of the grass, bluets
and mayflowers and violets. Some I cut,
others I work my way around.
My son wants to help rake, but soon
realizes that even for extra allowance
it's a lot of work in the sun, the rake
is long and the day is short.
He runs off and I am left with my
huge lawn, making patterns with the mower.
Each cut determines the next, a gentle
curve, a loopy rectangle, a straight line.
The morning paper tells me Yogi Berra
and Krishnamurti are also born on this day.
These wise men join me on my walk
through the grass, Yogi still in uniform
his arm on my shoulder, Krishnamurti,
a little more removed, walks with his
hands clasped behind his back. You are free
whenever your mind is free he tells me.
It's not over 'til it's over, Yogi joins in.
So we walk back and forth cutting our way,
lost in conversation, the deep earth
beneath our every step.

X Ray

The bone that dreams beneath the skin
longs for the light to pass through it,
to show its smooth surface, its corona
of sockets, its lunar essence. All day

you labor to discover what is inside you
and here it is: not just an idea, but
the very framework that has supported you
all these years, buried

beneath the muscle its many lives:
the cows in the field, the grass
in the sun, the grain swaying
back and forth under the moon-lit sky.

Birds, Like Ideas, Appear Out of Nowhere

First the blue jays
four of five of them,
pecking in syncopation
at the fallen seed.
Then the purple finch
appears with a breast
like a blush
a thought you didn't
mean to have, and takes
sustenance from the tall
cylindrical feeder.

And when I turn to do
something else and then
look back, a woodpecker,
bold black, white, and red
looking like a player from
a team I've never seen
in a bright home uniform.
These birds, like ideas,
appear out of nowhere,
I turn and they are there,
coming to the feeders
out of the blue air, out
of the thicket by the old
unpruned apple trees,
out behind the granite
boulders, out of the spruce
wood where the snow shakes
free from the branches
when they depart.

I Look Toward Heaven the Way a Dog Looks at a Door

Lying down, head resting on paws,
he stares with brown eyes, doggy
eyebrows furrowed and twitching,
at the edge of the door
where the light streams in
or at the golden knob
waiting for it to turn.
A dog doesn't control doors
but he knows they are
objects of significance.
He knows that if he stares long enough
something will happen. If dogs
had a religion, they would worship
the door, the same way that
if cats had a religion
they would worship the can opener.

Eventually the door will open,
his master will be there
to take him for a walk, or
better yet, he will slip the leash
and run through the dark forest,
looking for mysterious
dead things to roll in.

He comes back home panting, exhausted.
All night his legs twitch while
his body remembers the deer
slipping through the spruce woods.
He whimpers in his sleep to no one in particular.
I've been there, he dreams, I've been there.

Waiting for the Word

Listening to the no school announcements
in the early morning dark,
following last night's storm,
which in the deep gray
of the snow falling sky,
seemed like it would last forever
as it hissed against the windows
and blew down from the roof.
The cats stayed close to the bed
one son had a nightmare
and the other was in my dream
where we hobbled down a broken city street
afraid of gunfire. And this morning
we listen to the babble of the djs
who are almost funny except
they don't really love or hate
anything they are talking about.

Finally they read the cancellations
school district after school district
the litany of towns bearing Indian names,
names of the first white settlers
or names that must have come
as visions or prayers— Hope, Unity, Freedom . . .
We wait to hear our town on the radio
to be sanctified over the air waves
with the blessing of no school.
No school, no day beginning
in the hibernating dark,
time to make one more dream, time without time.

November Landscape

1

I stalk down the aisle
careful not to crunch on dried leaves,
following the footprints left where the store clerks
have mopped up a wet spill on aisle five
and make my way down
to the back of the store.
I crawl up to the round window
and scratch the frost away with my fingernail
so I can see inside.
The butchers are slaughtering
the chickens, the cows, the pigs,
the entrails make a marsh of blood on the floor.
Men are stripped to the waist
and have painted one another's faces
with the blood pigment. They make offerings
to the animals, place grain in front
of their mouths, wish them
a safe journey to the other world.
They pray before they slit the throat.
One of the men pushes through the door
to restock the shelves. He sees I have a gun
and tosses the styrofoam package in the air.
It is like a bird in flight
and I plug it in the sky,
the bullet passes through the meat
misses the fluorescent lights
and pierces the suspended ceiling.
I head toward the checkout,
the wheels of the cart click like a drumbeat
in rhythm with my pounding heart,
the ancient song.

November Landscape

2

The next morning
there has been a frost in the field.
I discover a deer carcass
in the spruce woods behind the house.
Fur surrounds the bones,
so that it looks like feathers,
like a pillow cut open and spread out.
The tongue is still attached
to the skeleton. We make a shrine
where we can listen to the mouth.
What will it tell us?
We put rocks around the body to remember
the glaciers that scoured the land.
Mice gnaw at the bones.
In winter I can follow tracks
of deer as they emerge
from the deeper woods to eat apples.
Generations of deer must travel
this animal highway at night
when we are inside, watching news
on the TV from around the world, wars everywhere,
the ice blue stars in the heavens.

This Is My Life It Is Here In This Moment

The ice rumbles and cracks along the narrow pond
as I lace up my hockey skates,
brown and black leather with the toes scuffed raw,
rust underneath where the blades attach, Salvation
Army skates, these fifty cent specials
nearly fit except where they cut me
just below my ankle bone.
I step on the ice, rippled in sections
like a sandy beach, the knees wobble
but hold, the ankles turn in slightly,
the shins ache at their new job.
Then I push off, left foot glide,
right foot glide. Ice a foot and a half thick
rumbles down the pond as it settles,
cracks criss-cross the surface, making
a record of these adjustments.
I see a green bottle trapped between layers,
like a message from a lost sailor,
stones and sticks embedded
after a thaw and a freeze.
I remember Houdini, who survived in a river
breathing the air in the space between
ice and water, listening to his mother's voice
calling him home. On the surface I am lurching
from skate to skate, but inside I am gliding
like a speed skater with bulging thighs.
Such smooth ice and I am the only skater on it.
All alone I race against spring
against my memory, my aging heart.
Soon my Olympic judges will hold up
their scoring cards or I will look at the clock
of my imagination to see my time. I am breathing heavily
holding my hands on my knees. The fish are
beneath me, a wind that has traveled
around the world meets my face.
I am walking on water.

Stepping Out of the Body

Like someone stepping
from a pair of dirty overalls,
turned inside out on the bathroom floor
I step from my body.
Words spill out, a pocket full of
nearly, almost, close, rattling on the ground.
I rise up and I am eye to eye
with the ceramic insulators on the power lines.
They glisten and I can see
a fish eye reflection
of the stony landscape and worn blacktop.
I touch the wire
and the current passes through me.
I float above the trees
like children's soap bubbles
on a spring day. Everyone I love
is below me. I see the tops of their heads
as they go about their business.
The school bus arrives
and swallows my children.
I am here about to join everything
the way bubbles burst
with a quiet pop, the tiny
strands of soap vanishing into the air.
There are souls all around me
pushing, pushing, there is the world
below me, caught by surprise in a spring storm.
There is the ocean embracing each rock.
I look down and can see
the inside of my skull,
the graffiti of dreams,
the rust of education.
Should I come back and inhabit this vehicle?
Under the sign at the Redemption Center
people are returning their bottles,
with the thin sour smell of beer and milk.
Do we re-use the vessel or do we
crush the can so it becomes something else.

Someone is embracing me
with both arms, whispering,
come home all is forgiven.
Am I coming or going?
Between this world
and the next all I can tell you this:
Something is about to be born.

I Am Fishing for God

using my heart as bait.
It is just before dawn,
the slightest hint of

pink bleeds into the
night sky. I use my
pen knife to cut the

hole in my chest,
reaching behind the
pocket of my shirt.

What a tough muscle
to pull the hook through.
The heart is astonished

to be in this other world
and trembles and shivers like
a moth discovered in daylight.

I try to calm it by stroking it
by telling it that it will all be
ok, but what do I know.

The breeze picks up and chills the cavern
in my chest. It feels good to
be empty at last. I cast my heart

across the water. I cast it again
and again. Sometimes it floats on
the surface, other times it sinks

below. Something will strike at it
that I can't see. I pray
I am using the right bait.

The tough outer layers
soften in the water. The heart grows
smaller, more pliant.

It has become a beautiful
blue jewel. I begin
not to recognize it.

Was this me?
It waits. I wait.
The boat rocks

slightly in the breeze
lifted and lowered
by the tide.

Landfill

The gulls still talk among themselves
of the golden days of the dump and how
it's not the same anymore
now that the garbage is being separated
and the unity of life is gone.

Still, they worship at this Church
of Re-Use and Decay, remembering when
they could dig into a plastic bag with their beaks
and pull out a twinkie or an apple as if it were
Christmas morning, and longing for

the days before the fish waste was turned
into compost and there would be a sacred mountain
of crab shells for the whole family.
I attend the same religious service,
heading off on the sabbath in the truck

to the shrines of the landfill where
everything that was us is here:
the sodden mattresses and recliners that held our dreams,
the burn pile where our old rooms are transformed
into flame and ash, the metals pile that is the anteroom

to rebirth, refrigerators, grates, and stoves
empty of use, waiting for the magnet.
I hear the sounds of my own goodness on the collection plate,
throwing the tin cans without labels,
newspapers, newspapers, newspapers, hdpe #2 plastic

no lids please into the recycling bins,
and then my final stop, the giant blue compactor
where I throw hefty bags of my past,
bank records and canceled checks,
twenty year old notebooks from the sociology course

I never liked and next week I swear I'll throw out
the old love letters and then the journals.
When the compactor is filled the big truck comes
and hauls it down to the trash-to-energy plant in
Orrington. There all the past is burned into

electricity and added to the power grid, so that
the computer I'm writing on now is running on something
you've thrown away and perhaps you're reading this
by a 60 watt bulb, the light generated by
my first drafts, old toothbrush, and last week's mail.

The Roads Not Taken

Two roads diverged in a yellow wood
and I being one traveler, etc. looked
down one road and I could see
junior high English teachers using
tambourines to beat out
the rhythm in poems. There were people
manufacturing posters with sayings on them,
like 'today is the first day
of the rest of your life.' There were
advertising executives thinking of
short sentences. Full. Of. Meaning.
I looked down the other road and
it was full of poets, writers
and artists all looking at one another.
Whoever planned this path
didn't figure there would be so many.
There was nothing to eat,
and they had stripped all the bushes
of berries and had begun to gnaw
at the tender bark of the saplings. You bet
I stood for a long time at that intersection
where I was surrounded by what was left
of the forest, the roots of the trees
probing each rock, embracing
each other's roots, knowing the wind
never ceases and water is religion.

Sabbath

I want us to make this pilgrimage every week:
After we have kindled the Sabbath candles,
walk away from the house and stand
in the back field, away from the road's
light and traffic, so that the stars become
brighter and we can look at our own house
for what it is—a shelter from the wilderness
that surrounds us, the ancient light of the
Milky Way and the steady beating of the wind
rattling ash and spruce. Endless wind, endless night,
a harmony so frightening we head back
into the house, pretending to be cold. Could we
add a minute each time to what we
can bear, so that years from now we will
stand there all night in the slow circling of heaven,
the Dipper emptying itself, the fox and deer
brushing against us as they make their rounds.

Essence

We hand-crank the drill through the maple's bark,
pound the metal tap into light inner layers

where the sap begins to flow, this life blood
that will make the leaves unfurl

in another two months, delicately
lined like the hands of a newborn.

But now we step over last year's leaves
and the year's before that

in patchy snow to gather what
we have taken from the tree, the gallons of sap

we boil down on our stove top,
moisture running off the kitchen windows

as we get down to its essence, over three gallons
to make a cup of syrup, so sweet

a transformation, I can't believe I could
have been a part of it. A world that doesn't

end in vinegar, ashes and regret,
but in a sweetness that rises every day

between earth and sky, traveling from the hole
in the side of the tree to our joyous mouths.

II

Today

It's not like you're trying to catch something
but if you don't make note of it, it's gone,

the conical shadow of the cedar moving
into itself near noon, the flies who weren't

alive yesterday, making a buzzing music in the sun.
The hum of the field and the bellowing of the cattle

up the mountain slope. Down the valley a rooster crows.
It crowed yesterday and will crow again, but now it crows,

now the shadows grow shorter and the eucalyptus leaves
hang in the breezeless afternoon. A poem is a sail

to a breeze picking up, a net that catches the fish.
It lets you know, suddenly, the world

is out there, thrashing outside of you. You fish
catch and release, you let this world swim back into

today's stream that is rushing over rocks,
that is reflecting the cloud swirling sky.

Radio

The dash board, always stuck underneath
the dash, only a front facing the world.

The body hidden inside, all circuits,
wire and solder. The body that wants

to eat wave after wave of spicy
electrons, the hot stuff of the air.

Oh it knows everyone wants to hear
the perfect song, the one that

sets the day right, but it is so
tired of everyone's idea of perfection

and the changing, the seasick rolling
from classical to country western and

back again, through advice on investments
and someone praising the lord. And the voices

of the dead still coming through it on tape.
All it wants is the undifferentiated sound,

the waves all gathering up, the frequencies
joined, the steady hum through the antenna.

Pencil Sharpener's Lament

I am a sword swallower, word after
potential word down my throat.
When the show's over I am left

with only the dust of what is written
the shavings that surround the poem.
Sure I live in fear of algebra as much

as the next guy. Think how many equations
and wrong answers I hold in my gut.
I have memorized and eaten motels, restaurants,

souvenir shops, and garages. These are
the places where I build my dream
that is always the same: something grinds

and turns inside me, a light snow is falling
and the mysterious world comes to me:
Dixon, Ticonderoga, #1, #2, #3.

Urinals

When I went on a tour of the Kohler factory
I walked into a 19th century industrial room
that was full of urinals, unfired and smelling
like the damp earth, the scent that fills
the memories of potters throughout time,
and saw one after another of this most humble
of objects, unglazed and gray,
an elegant shape still without function,
the curved back that no one ever sees
when it is mounted on a tiled wall
of the airport or movie theater, but now
I never look at these vessels the same way
as I take aim wherever commerce is,
wherever travelers go. The urinal,
where I can shred a cigarette butt or
disintegrate a disinfectant disk. And so many
models: the trough, the down to the floor,
low to the ground for kids, automatic flusher,
all these vessels that carry our water
in the public restroom, millions of flushes,
men sending cups of coffee, morning juice,
wine and beer and all those illusions
as we stand in a trance, staring at the glazed surface,
a moment without time, holding on to our penises,
thinking, is this what I was meant to be,
pouring ourselves into this simple vessel,
that holds beauty you can't see
that once smelled like the earth
and was transformed by fire, that knows what it's
there for and therefore knows what it is.

The Metered Life

The moment you slide into the back seat of the taxi
you know life is measured, the dollars

on the meter already, and then every quarter mile,
half mile, every extended wait bumper to bumper

adding to the fare. You can look at the driver's
registration, his photo, learn what your rights are,

look at Manhattan blur on either side, but
your eyes are fixed on the red numbers,

the bill you're running up. Other parts
of your life, you never see the cost as

directly. Here you're driven a mile, you spend
money, watch it go yard by yard. But why

only taxis? Why not the metered life
for everything, the digital read out

on your phone telling you those minutes
with your mother are costing you, and why not

one above the television, one attached to
the plumber's back like a scoreboard,

or one on each shoe letting you know
each step has a price. How about a meter for

the paint wearing off your house, or one on each
child letting you know what it costs to raise them.

Wouldn't that keep your life in line, knowing what
each day costs, and you could reach into your pocket

at nightfall and settle up. Now in some places
like Washington, DC the cabs don't have meters,

you drive through mysterious zones that only
the driver knows and he lets you know the total.

There's some trust involved there, waiting until the end to find out
what you owe, fumbling with your wallet as the traffic hums by.

Central Square

When I emerge from the T
on an early March morning, wind blowing
so hard that a page from the *Herald*
has taken flight and is floating above
the cars and intent pedestrians.
At first it flutters with a flock of pigeons
and then soars off on its own,
three or four stories in the air.
The tallest building in the square
stands in the wind, cumulus clouds scudding
over its roof, so that against the blue sky
the building moves like a boat
in a sea of white caps. I suppose the truth
of it is that we are all moving, holding
on to our dear Earth with gravity's feet.
I can almost read what the page of the sailing
newspaper says, as if the headline were written
to me. We can always turn everything
into messages for ourselves. I send off
a prayer in this strong wind, only it circles
back around me again and again, a cyclone
of the heart's calligraphy.

Laughter

You know the kind of laughter
when you laugh so hard and unexpectedly
you can snort liquid right through
your nose, like the soda you were drinking.
That's what happened to me with a milkshake
when I was 11 years old and too worried
for my own good. My uncle and I were swapping
book jokes. "Have you read *Tiger's Revenge*
by Claude Balls?" he asks, which strikes me
as so funny that I begin to laugh
uncontrollably and milk is dripping from my nose
almost like I've thrown up, but instead
I feel incredibly light and happy.
That's the kind of laughter that even
if you have been crying and heard someone
else laughing, you would start to laugh.
It spreads like a wind passing
through leaves, it makes the bitter muscle
of the heart unclench itself. Imagine,
all this from only eight words from my uncle,
and one of those a preposition
with only two letters.

III

Carrying It On

My children climb into bed with me
and yank out the gray hairs they find,
trying to eliminate these early warning signs
of mortality. My father, may he rest in peace,

had gray hair and his father before him.
Now they are gone, not even 150 years
between them. Even my great grandmother, who crossed
a stormy Atlantic to reach the New World,

was not alive 200 years ago,
and no one today was living when
Moses stuttered the commandments or
Chuang Tzu dreamed he was a butterfly.

It's amazing how we keep dying
and still know all that we do,
our knowledge like a train riding
on glistening rails, where we

eavesdrop from our seats to learn
enough of the ancient conversation to
carry our story on. We'll get off,
but more newcomers will be listening.

The passengers who have disembarked
stand under the deep blue evening
when the train pulls away. They look
at one another and smile and
begin new tales. All around them are

posted the old stories, like billboards
for a circus that has left. The train
goes around another curve, barreling
recklessly forward, rattling with light.

When I Was Ten I Had a Prayer Answered

The fireflies send their yellow beacons
into the humid New Jersey air
as dusk surrounds each house
pushing its way through our screen windows,
mingling with the blue light of the TV.
In this glow we sit watching
the Yankees play the Detroit Tigers.
It's an away game, so even as the sky
begins to rumble, in Michigan
the lights haven't come on yet.
I love Mickey Mantle with a passion.
I know when he was born, what's wrong with his knees,
how great he is, and how he still isn't
as great as he could be.
He steps up to bat as the thunder and lightning
begin in our suburban sky. I send off a prayer
for the Mick as Mel Allen updates his batting average.
Oh dear God, let him hit a home run.
He's got bad knees, he's from Oklahoma,
his father is dead… let him do well,
thinking all this quickly and fervently
so that it will be sent before the pitch
arrives at the plate. And his bat connects
and the ball sails into the stands of Tiger Stadium.

How did this one small prayer
find its way into heaven so quickly?
How did it rocket past the prayers of children
sick with malaria in the UNICEF films, the old women
next to their husbands in the metallic white wards
of Beth Israel hospital, past the prayers of my
next door neighbor whose mother died
of cancer, past all the prayers
of the children in concentration camps,
a forest of eyes behind unscalable fences.
So many prayers they must
have sent up, so many unanswered.
The prayers cling to the Gates of Heaven

like butterflies, wings trembling in the celestial breeze
made every time a soul breaks free.

What was God thinking to let mine in and
leave the other ones at the Gate.
A homerun, that's an easy one,
let the kid have it. And the
uncountable prayers on the way up
fighting through the thick air,
so many it sounds like a swarm of bees in spring,
a desperate hum of hope. Mickey circles the bases
on his bum knees. Outside thunder rolls and
the rain begins, raining hard, pounding on
the windows and the shining black street.

Breaking Free

I am pledging allegiance to the flag
in the basement classroom when
my crewcut friend appears at the door
with a message. He whispers to the teacher

who motions to me, and I learn that
my dog has followed me to school.
What an occasion, that above all the other
scents in the world, all the other

high-topped sneakers, he has found me out.
I learn that he has already made it through
the first grade, where he has
muddied a teacher's dress with his dark paws.

I imagine his journey as he runs down
the long corridors that smell of chalk dust
and institutional cleanser, cantering
past the principal's office, the holy of holies,

where the records are kept. I see him sniffing
at the blunt toed shoes of the army
of teachers who find him.
He wags his tail when he sees me, but I am

overcome with my notoriety. Why did you
follow me, why single me out? I get the dog
and put him out the front entrance.
Go home, I tell him, go on home, ignoring

his optimistic eyes, shutting
the great wooden doors
on that part of me that is
without a collar and wild.

Knowledge

My teachers gave me subjects to research for reports.
In that way I came to know about certain things:
fog, geraniums, Wisconsin, and even now have a certain
fondness for these topics as if they belonged to me
because I looked them up in the World Book Encyclopedia

and paraphrased its contents. I feel similarly about
the Battle of Tours, tortillas and the solar system.
I was not just a student of these topics, it's as if we were
in some way friends. But I didn't have such an easy relationship
with map reading at least on the Iowa Test of Basic Skills.

After my mother came back from the conference with my teacher
she said I must have been confused when I read the instructions.
What else can a mother say?
Either way I am able to get almost anywhere I want to go now.
And if I wasn't that bright about the map, I sure made up for it

when I traded with my friend, giving him a large wooden yo-yo
that couldn't climb up the string for his pencil box with two
rotating dials, one with the name of the state, the other
with the capital. Try me even now... North Dakota? Bismarck.
Nevada? Carson City. Washington? Olympia! Imagine my thrill

at driving through Trenton and seeing the sign over the bridge,
Trenton Makes the World Takes. My pencil box had come to life.
Because I knew their names these were all my cities,
the glistening domes of the capitols, the workers
in the long brown corridors with the names of the departments

painted on the smoked glass of the closed doors.
Even now I can imagine Des Moines, Iowa where a man
is making up a test. Another is making little circles.
Someone else is filling them in with a new #2 pencil,
the rich darkness of the answer, right or wrong.

Religion

With a heavy Yiddish accent
our immigrant teacher told us
stories from the Bible
where I would freely integrate
New Jersey with the ancient and holy desert.
So when she told us that two
angels disguised as men
visited Sarah and Abraham in their
old age, I could see
these bearers of good news going
door to door, the relentless
sun beating down on them,
only they looked more like private eyes
with trench coats or the Fuller Brush Man
who had escaped from Germany.
Now you know Sarah laughed
when she heard she would bear
a child in old age and I'm sure
she was also laughing a little
at these visitors I'd sent from another time
who spoke Aramaic with an accent from Newark
just as these men were startled to
find themselves talking in another language,
the word of God breaking through
the after dinner silence in the tent
whose interior looked remarkably
like the apartment of my grandmother,
a woman who had her own stories,
the oldest person I knew.

Vasectomy

I know that I won't be calling
on those tireless swimmers anymore

to make the arduous journey up the love canal.
The narrow tube that carries the family

to the ocean has admirably fulfilled its function,
turning ecstasy into consequence and now just like

the happy couple pictured in front of the glowing fire
in the informational pamphlet, I'll be gaining new freedom

anywhere anytime, anywhere anytime, still
when I kiss my sons good-bye in the morning

and head off for the outpatient clinic,
I can't help when I smell their hair

to marvel at this issue, the seed that has been
sown for the last time. I know these children

are the gateway to immortality, but I grow
increasingly more mortal as I take off

my clothes and slip into the hospital johnnie
and wear the plastic bracelet with my name and age

and when I'm being operated on, more like a car
on the lift than anything else, the mechanic

pulling out the color-coded wiring, one vehicle
not that much different from the rest, ah but

to the owner, there are the memories
of the first drives, the spring days

with the windows rolled down, the soft air
in your face the warm earth ready for planting.

Dark

I lie down with my son at bedtime,
full moon illuminating the apple trees
in white flower, the lilac fragrance
ascending through the open window.
Such a short burst of heat,
and we are in a blossoming world.
How quickly it will go by,
first the apple, then the lilacs,
then peonies, irises... He wants me
to lie down with him because
he's afraid of being alone in the dark,
and who wouldn't be, with so much life outside.
An evening star glitters like a piece
of broken glass on the beach.
Earlier the red clouds filled
the vast domed world to the west.
The west, where I used to imagine
cowboys who rode out from town on horseback
watching the sun slipping into the earth,
its home for the night.
Now I know it's never home, it
races around and around, and even as I am here
drifting off in the dark before
my son falls asleep, it is showering
some place I don't know with light,
baffling, inevitable light.

First Love Lost

The photo booth four shots for a dollar,
photo in minutes, the masonite sides with fake
wood grain finish, the photos that emerge stinking

and nearly resembling you. The booth squats
in the train station where arrivals and departures
echo off the marble floors and heroic murals.

You want to kill time and drop in four quarters,
time to find out who you are, boy becoming a man.
There is no growth of beard yet to show for the long day

hitchhiking, the bus rides, telling strangers your
story as if your life were the only story to tell.
And the photos come out black, no light has etched

your image, and coated with chemical residue,
the way your life is now coated with sorrow
that clings to you as you board the train

where you observe yourself, floating
outside the window, your own partner
in darkness for the ride home.

The First Snowfall

The first snowfall
is a single memory,
the thin residue
of a dream, all the
outlines defined,
empty spacious air that says
something else is coming.
The crows scream
black warnings into gray silence
and the wind spirals and blows
the snow across the sky
parallel to the ground,
making dashes of Morse code,
indecipherable fragments.
Whenever the first snowfall comes
I remember the first snows
of college, the heat coming
up in the classrooms with
yellowed wooden floors, the radiators
knocking and coughing, like an old
smoker getting up in the morning.
And the professors on their
hands and knees blowing
on the embers of civilization
hoping for another year it will all
flame up in our minds. They watch
as Socrates dies again and our
sentences become more and more
perfect. Walking across the paths
with so many ideas swirling, in the
icy world of tradition and the snow
beginning to fall, always falling,
as if it were the first time
it had ever come as if
when I die it will be
the first time anyone has.

Guest Room

We always kept snapshots
in an old shoe box, not an album,
so every descent into the past was
an archeological dig through family history.
Generations were entwined, making fathers into sons,
and dead into the living. How many more years
before you and I are only photographs,
at first fondly remembered
and then added to the confusion,
mistaken for a cousin or a brother.

In the guest room at my mother's
we are surrounded by these images on the walls,
nieces and nephews eternally in elementary school
my recently engaged grandparents
by lamplight, looking toward a long-gone future.
All those eyes looking on us
as we sleep on the fold out couch.
Dare we make love with so many watching?

At dawn I stir and find
I am sleeping with my front to your back,
my hand cups your breast
and I feel your heart flutter
right into my palm,
over the beat of my own pulse.
How delicate, holding this
fragile bird in my hands.
Where does it rest? Where does it fly to?
We only know that it will fly from us and
this is a story whose end we can't change,
but we can make up the middle,
the improvisations of
our tongues, all the new languages
we learn to speak.

Awake

for my sons, Isaac and Sam

If, when I see you,
your head against
the pillow, body turned
from dreaming, and listen
for your breath, the same way
I would listen when you
were first born to hear
the lungs' sweet air
while you slept,
then waking you now
I can forget a father's sedimentary
mistakes and the future
careening forward like an
out of control car
on an icy road, I can forget
everything except our hearts
beating in the same room,
the pulse between us.

Remembrance

I place a stone
of memory on my father's grave
wipe the marker clean
of the residue of fallen leaves.

I see that the grave is
heaved up higher than
the place reserved
for my mother,

a mound that reminds me
of his barrel chest.
We don't talk as much as
acknowledge each other in this

spring morning when the daffodils
make yellow gestures of hope
in the awakening grounds.
Each flower remembers,

but it remembers only for
the first time. Or is it
the plant that remembers
and the flower that is

the celebration of memory or
is it the earth that remembers
and wakes up the plant
or do the roots have a dim

memory, like a family
sitting around a dining room table
after a holiday meal, pushing
back their chairs, a little too full.

A conversation begins
and the uncle's recollection
turns into the sister's memory
into the child's dream

back to the grandmother vanishing
into the white so white table cloth
stained with those things
that feed us while we are here.

The Light

A Camel-smoking teenager I have just returned
from New York City with my friend
Ellen, she of the wispy blonde
hair in her eyes and the sophisticated
laugh, when a moth dives deep
into my throat, so that I can't
talk or swallow. We are on the way
to her house, for what I pray will be
love and I can't even tell her
what has happened, I just
stand there in the mercury vapor
light on South Orange Avenue
until we part and I walk home.
The day in New York with the visits
to her genteel friends,
the Metropolitan Museum of Art,
and Art Students League and the
exotic promise of the train station
all behind us, I knew I just wanted
a girl to put in my life to make
me whole and instead I swallow
a moth, the brown and white
moth that circles endlessly around
the glow, that can burn itself on the
candle of desire. It must have been
after the light that was
inside me, the light that
even after all these years
I have not yet seen or understood.

IV

Day Job

Sometimes I would get to make the salads,
and one time I accidentally dropped
a wine glass into the ice machine
where it broke into indistinguishable slivers

that I cleaned out though I still couldn't help imagining
the customers' intestines bleeding when they
got home, stuffed and bloated after their fine
Italian meal. But mostly I was washing the dishes

scrubbing the casseroles again and again,
occasionally eating untouched shrimp scampi
from the plates the came back in and made
the traffic jam of dishes that lay before me.

What did I know about work, only that
I didn't want to be the one left alone
in the kitchen at night, after the wild cook
and the sturdy assistant cook went home,

after the waitresses went home with their
aprons full of gratuities, and the cocktail waitresses
came up from the bar downstairs, dollars woven around
their sexy fingers, looking for change for their patrons.

I couldn't help them with money, I still had a floor to wash
and the enormous pot sink to get to. I was always eager
to go on a break and smoke a cigarette at the window,
which overlooked a church on Mellon Street.

At sunset, by design or by accident, that summer sun
would blaze on the crosses of the steeples
so that it looked as if they had ignited. Then back to the dishes,
and if they were done, on to the toilets or cleaning the floor.

A holy man wrote that a form of meditation
is to wash each dish as if God were coming to dinner.
With what care and awe I could have
scrubbed and shined each plate and bowl.

And who knows what was out in the dining room,
outside those swinging doors where the distorted
rumble of conversation makes itself into an unknown tongue,
sentences like the endless flow of water.

After *Man Waiting For Dark, Juarez, Mexico*

—*photograph by Paul D'Amato*

The man waits in his truck, the sun hasn't gone down yet
and you can see the last rays of the light, golden light that falls
only across his elbow resting on the door of the old van
and across his face as if the light has chiseled it.

It's not the light that has created this face,
its reddish beard and brown eyes, but the confluence
of Spanish and Aztec, a record of how violence leads
to creation and our language changes so that eventually

we are speaking in a tongue we weren't born with.
Travel around the world and it will always come down
to this: somebody has taken over from somebody else,
and still our world goes on. We buy candy and aspirin

at the *farmacia*, we sweeten our lives and ease our pain,
the air is filled with the exhaust of our idling vehicles.
In the windshield you can see the reflection
of the power lines overhead, connecting us to each other.

Within the wires the flow of electrons that will keep
our world lit even as the sun descends behind
the hot and tired leaves of the rustling trees. For a minute
longer the sunlight is in the eyes of the man at the wheel,

at that moment of the day when it's not the middle of the day
and you think the light will be with you forever but the end
of the day, when too soon the light is gone and a cool breeze
blows in from the silent desert, across the worn stones of your heart.

House of Thanksgiving

In the house of thanksgiving
I have seen the angels late at night,
the incandescent light still on downstairs.
They are writing psalms with quills

they pull from their wings.
They toss crumpled drafts into the woodstove
and smoke rises from the chimney,
still holding the shape of the words,

then feathers out into a gray landscape.
The soot makes a film on the shrubs.
These angels sing their songs of praise
until they have moved past irony

into full-on love and kiss one another
with passion, and become like children
at a family gathering,
running from room to joyous room

in the circle of downstairs.
If I watch them all night, at dawn
I see the birch branches shaking in lavender light
like fine capillaries where this world flows into the next

and if I step outside my own house
I can hear them laughing
and hear the heavy thud
of their footsteps in prayer.

House of Mourning

There is only the damp stone darkness—
no light at first, just the sound of the women

wailing, which begins as a low moan that grows
to a howl, as if time and again

they are building a wind out of grief.
They are the ones who give birth

to the ones who suffer and so make this ancient
music for the children, the brothers,

the soldiers who die for nothing
or something. If you look up

to the few high windows, you can see
bare apple branches or the delicate white

flowers in spring trembling slightly against a sky
full of rain. Rain makes a muted sound

against the slate roof and runs down
the stone walls as if each drop were a river

carving a canyon of loss. There are no
men to be seen, they are outside

with their shovels, burying someone or
planting seeds, calling on the earth,

one way or the other. The women
walk out to join them in these fields

miles of treeless landscape spreading out
to the horizon. The horizon

where days begin and end, and sorrow
approaches from all directions.

House of Prayer

Inside the house of prayer the ancient ones
rock slowly back and forth,
they have been praying since just after time began,
when the sun, new itself, rose on the first day

after humans were created. Even way back then
there were fervent wishes. The path to the house
is worn and rutted, outside the barn
are two silos full of prayers,

a satellite dish with channels upon channels
for sending and receiving.
Bales of old prayers bank the foundation for winter.
Over time the broken and the restless make pilgrimages,

each with their own hearts to pray for.
Inside it is nearly silent, except for the faint
sound of lips moving and an occasional moan
of sorrow or remembrance.

And then there are the prayers
that get jumbled, like leaving the right phone message
on the wrong answering machine,
only you don't know it and can't take it back.

This is what has happened throughout time.
It gives us what sympathy we have.
Don't search for your own prayer
with your name sewn in the back,

don't try to find the pure thought
that danced from your lips.
Think of the person who wanted what you've gotten.
Think of healthy children, plentiful food.

Think of a man in another country,
who can finally weep,
who is watching the sun rise
on the only day there is.

House of Horrors

The house of horrors has been re-sided a few times.
First it was clapboards, then asphalt shingles, and finally
aluminum siding covering all the architectural detail

of this fine old home that once belonged
to a family, then became a doctor's office until
the neighborhood changed. Today there are rooms

full of computers that store all the data
of every terror to date. In fact, today they are switching over
to a networked system, so that if you are responsible

for Bosnia, you don't have to walk over to
the caseworker for Auschwitz, and "Incest, rural"
and "Incest, urban" can communicate with just

a few strokes of the keyboard. Technology changes
so quickly. The old terminals, which everyone thought
were such a marvel, now seem slow and antiquated,

their plastic cases yellowed and cracked. The new system
will be virtually paperless, so there won't be
nagging problems of misplaced records or the overworked

secretary who takes files home only to have them turn up
months after, tear stained, with grocery lists scrawled on the back.
They've been throwing the paper files out the window

into a dumpster in the back yard. Pity the poor flower beds
in what used to be the garden as a box misses the mark,
box upon box, centuries of atrocities each day. In the alley

behind the yard day laborers are burning
the papers in a fifty-five-gallon drum, keeping warm,
soot blowing down the deserted street.

House of Remembrance

The walls are lined with disintegrating newsclips,
snapshots with color fading, granite plaques carved
with family histories. Lips and fingers have rubbed

away parts of words and faces, new stories are layered
on old ones like beech leaves on a forest floor. During the day
people come from the street to this silent refuge,

pin another photograph to the wall, drop
a dollar in the box, and light a candle for the altar.
In the evening no one is here except

for the caretaker who is napping
comforted by the sputtering candles.
He is woken by the scratching

of dry snow against dirty windows.
He begins his rounds, walking down
the corridors leading to the older rooms:

caves of dark fire, desert wind, spring rain.
He runs his hands along the wall, no alarm system,
no please do not touch.

The Body Remembers

I slip on the rocks at low tide
floating for a timeless moment

over the skeletons of shells, the fields
of barnacles, until my face meets the granite

and my cheek and eye
grow numb and turn blue

and black as my body sets about to heal
the damaged tissue, the broken bone.

To think all this is programmed inside me,
never called on until this moment of swelling

and bleeding. My body, my faithful companion,
my inside out, my outside in, repairs itself

while I sit on top of it, like some incompetent
ruler whose aides know how to take care of all the details.

My body mends itself, like a fisherman at his nets,
like my mother-in-law darning socks. Our job on earth

is to repair the broken and bruised world.
We fix from within, we pull into the garage of the soul

and put ourselves on the lift, take out
the wrenches and grease gun and get to work.

O miraculous recovery!
O what we don t know that blesses us!

The Other Shore

I stand at the edge of the Atlantic
and hold my father's hand. The ocean
is enormous, the ribbons of waves
break one after another over the jetties.
A wave can knock me down
and drag me for a terrifying
moment in the foam until I surface,
knees scraped by stones and coarse sand.
I ask my father what's on the other side.
Europe, he tells me, and I look out
to the horizon and see what must be
deep sea fishing boats and tankers headed
for port, and I turn their hulls
into the coast of the Netherlands, where people
lining the other shore wear colorful outfits
and wooden shoes and wave to me.
In that moment I discovered
that there was a larger world,
although one in which everyone
seemed to know who I was.
There are so many oceans,
so many shores. My father has
gone now, over to another shore,
too far away to see, where the water
is roiled by wind. Everyday boats arrive,
long white hulled boats whose oarsmen
effortlessly pull through the waves.

Returning Home I Dream I See My Father Again

When I walk in the back door
past the refrigerator and into the kitchen
you are sitting there in a ribbed undershirt
and gray work pants. Your day is done

but you are not tired. I bring you all my
treasures in a cigar box—the perfect
cat's eye marble, blue sea glass, broken
tile from the old neighbor's demolished house

matches from some thin-walled motel
in a faraway state. I have placed these
in a box for you to discover, to examine
each one and see why I love

the distance, the light, the strange
beauty of transformation that these
objects hold. Where have you been?
you would ask. In hiding places

in the green dreams of backyards,
in the melancholy world behind garages,
where secrets are told and children cry.
You would examine every piece with reverence

and tell a story about each one
making us laugh and be full
of pity for each small life, for the sidewalk
outside our house, for the maps inside

the glove compartment, for the acorns
that litter the yard, fallen from the world's
largest oak that pushes through our driveway,
for the neighbor's restless child

hoping for sleep. We watch the night
come on as we sit at the table, the fireflies'
yellow signals flickering on and off in the backyard
like distant lanterns from another kingdom.

Early June 2002, Deer Isle, Maine

We weren't waiting for anything to happen.
Just like geologists we were looking backward

at what already had: the molten granite pushing
its way from one hundred miles beneath the earth's surface to here

where it became an island only ten thousand years ago,
the top of a mountain suddenly surrounded

by the waters of the last ice age. And what's
ten thousand years compared to a geological epoch but

the blink of an eye. Some days can feel like that.
I rise and wander into my sons' rooms to wake them,

get them ready for school, each school year its own
sedimentary geology of projects and holidays,

bus rides and lunches, until finally it's spring
and the windows are open.

The screened world is re-discovered
and everything is blossoming all at once:

lilacs, apples, lupines and poppies, everywhere
bees coated in the pollen of survival.

A white curtain inhales the breeze and on the counter
six peonies in a yellow vase.

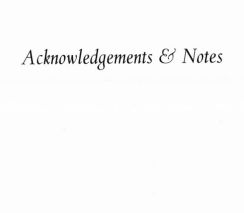

Acknowledgements & Notes

Acknowledgement is due to the editors of the following publications, in whose pages some of the poems in this book first appeared.

X Ray (Black Fly Review)
Birds Like Ideas Appear Out of Nowhere (Black Fly Review)
Fishing for God (Beloit Poetry Journal)
When I Was Ten I Had a Prayer Answered (Tikkun)
Post Office Box (Preview)
I Look Toward Heaven the Way a Dog Looks at a Door (wordplay)
Waiting for the Word (Belfast Republican Journal)
House of Prayer (The Sun)
House of Thanksgiving (The Sun)
House of Horrors (The Sun)
Sabbath (The Sun)
The Light (The Sun)
Returning Home I Dream I See My Father Again (The Sun)
Knowledge (The Sun)
Stepping Out of the Body (The Sun)
Vasectomy (Northeast Corridor)
Urinals (Northeast Corridor)
Cider (Maine Times)
Breaking Free (Maine Times)
Essence (Maine Times)
Remembrance (Puckerbrush Review)

Thanks to Bill Carpenter, Wesley McNair, and Betsy Sholl for reading the manuscript in various stages, and to my wife Susan and sons Isaac and Sam for their wisdom and encouragement.

Stuart Kestenbaum grew up in Maplewood, New Jersey and received a B.A. degree from Hamilton College. He has lived in Maine for many years and since 1988 has been the director of the Haystack Mountain School of Crafts in Deer Isle. He is also the author of Pilgrimage (Coyote Love Press). He is married to visual artist Susan B. Webster and they have two children, Isaac and Samuel.